Jesus Washes Peter's Feet

The Story of Jesus Washing the Disciple's Feet
John 13:1–12 for children

Written by Glynis Belec
Illustrated by Unada Gliewe

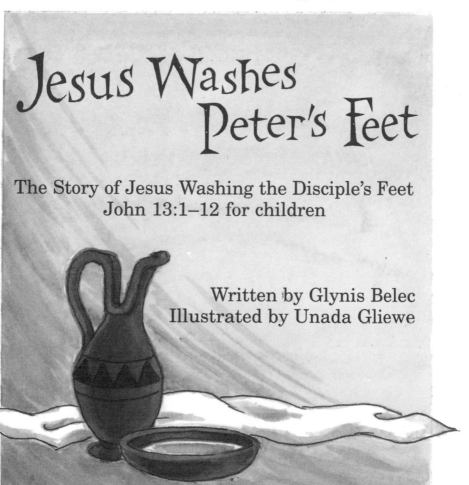

Arch® Books
Copyright © 2001 Concordia Publishing House
3558 S. Jefferson Avenue, St. Louis, MO 63118-3968
Manufactured in Colombia .

Jesus loved His disciples so much,
But He knew what had to be done;
Soon He would die and rise again
To finish the work He'd begun.

So on Thursday night He ate with His friends—
His last meal—but none of them knew.
Jesus quietly got up from the table.
They watched, wondering what He would do.

He wrapped a towel around His waist
And poured water into a large bowl.
He humbly knelt to wash each man's feet,
But self-glory was not Jesus' goal.

(You see, it was part of a servant's job
To greet all the guests at the door.
The roads were dusty; their feet would be soiled,
So they'd take off the sandals they wore.

And a bowl and towel would be ready—
For hosts wanted to offer their best.
Their servants would wash the dusty feet
Of each tired and weary guest.)

Jesus was tending to physical needs
As He stooped to wash His friends' feet.
But much more important than washing dirt
Were the spiritual needs He would meet.

For clothed in a towel around His waist,
He was taking a servant's part.
Jesus was teaching His friends that night
How to serve with a humble heart.

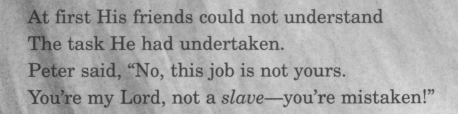

At first His friends could not understand
The task He had undertaken.
Peter said, "No, this job is not yours.
You're my Lord, not a *slave*—you're mistaken!"

Jesus looked up as a humble slave might
And told Peter, "I must do this task.
If you don't allow Me to wash your feet,
Then nothing from Me, can you ask!"

Looking at Jesus and seeing the love
Peter said, "Lord, not just my feet ...
Wash both my hands and the rest of me,
Please make my cleansing complete!"

Jesus said cleansing would not be needed;
Their bodies were already clean.
"Although," He said, "there *is* someone here
Who never will know what that means."

He was talking about His betrayer,
Though He did not point him out
Because He knew for God's Word to come true,
Crucifixion must be carried out.

Then when He finished washing their feet,
Jesus dressed and returned to His place.
He asked them, "Do you understand?"
Each looked at His serious face.

"I have given you an example.
Now go out and do the same:
Humble yourself, and serve with pure love,
Show devotion, and honor My name."

Now we can also serve Jesus,
And in humble submission we pray,
"Help us dear Lord to serve others
And follow Your example each day."

Dear Parents,

Having loved His own who were in the world, [Jesus] now showed [the disciples] the full extent of His love (John 13:1b). These words open the biblical account of this story. Jesus took on this menial task to emphasize humility, and to provide an example of selfless service that He would soon demonstrate on the cross. Jesus loves with a selfless, sacrificial love.

Do you think His disciples fully understood the meaning behind Jesus' actions? Most likely not, for they did not know or understand that Jesus was getting ready to take the eternal punishment for sin upon His shoulders. But *we* know the end of the story— we know that Jesus overcame eternal death and sin. He overcame it with selfless, sacrificial love.

[Jesus said,] "I have set you an example that you should do as I have done for you (John 13:15).
Out of love, thanksgiving, and gratitude, we follow the example of Jesus through humble service to others. What can you do to show the love of Jesus to someone else today?

The Editor